How to
Motivate,
Train and
Nurture

Acolytes

FIVE WORKSHOPS
AND OTHER RESOURCES

Morehouse Publishing
4775 Linglestown Road
Harrisburg, PA 17112

ISBN: 0-8192-0003-4

Printed in the United States of America

Table of Contents

Foreword

Acolyte training is a dynamic, ongoing process that evolves as acolytes enter and grow in their ministry. This book was written in response to a need for a manual that will help adults who work with acolytes discover creative ways to teach skills, encourage teamwork, and provide a strong spiritual foundation. It is not intended to be a handbook for acolytes, because they generally need more support and guidance than they would get from reading on their own. The book's intent is to suggest a flexible and responsive program, based on the premise that there is no one "best way" to work with acolytes, because they have to be prepared to serve within the wide variety of traditions and practices found among churches and clergy and across denominations

Drawn on experience from many parishes, diocesan acolyte gatherings, and various training workshops, this book is offered as a working tool. It presents concepts that will be helpful to people working with acolytes, and ideas for workshop-type training sessions that can be used as the foundation for acolyte training in any congregation. The sessions will work for any size group and are appropriate for trainers with varying levels of skill and experience. Although this manual is focused primarily on the needs and styles of adolescent acolytes, girls and boys and men and women of all ages are interested in the acolyte ministry, so suggestions can easily be adapted as needed.

We hope you find this manual helpful. Revisions will be made from time-to-time, so we would welcome your ideas and observations as you use the book in your acolyte training program. For your convenience several "tools" can be found in the Appendices, including a basic glossary, and a form for prayer and reflection that we suggest acolytes use regularly as they prepare to serve. Trainers also might find it enriching.

Although the book is written from the perspective of the Episcopal Church, the ideas and concepts can easily be translated to meet the requirements of other traditions. However, because of its Episcopal focus, you will see occasional references to material in *The Book of Common Prayer* (BCP).

An interesting road lies ahead. Good luck as you traverse it, and have fun!

THE ACOLYTE MINISTRY

The acolyte ministry is one of service. The theology and significance of this ministry should be reinforced through all phases of training. Acolytes of all ages and experience levels will benefit by constant encouragement about the value of their personal ministry in the Lord's service. Acolytes, along with other lay ministers in the Episcopal Church, are responsible for carrying out their ministry according to the questions and answers found in the Catechism on page 855 in the BCP.

Enthusiastic participation in the acolyte group and committed involvement to the acolyte ministry should be a primary goal of the program since it is key to the program's success. Efforts to establish that enthusiastic spirit should begin when a boy, girl, man, or woman first expresses interest in serving.

Clergy and acolyte directors often wonder about the best way to involve a new acolyte. Leaders should be clear that a regular training program, which will provide a level of comfort and security, will be part of the ministry. Then the acolyte can be introduced to service in whatever way is appropriate for your situation.

> Example: a new acolyte might be assigned a simple task and shepherded by an experienced peer, or could be scheduled for several sequential Sundays as a vested observer with an advanced acolyte as a mentor.

However you decide to encourage initial participation, it should be understood as a first step, leading to training that will enable the new acolyte to feel confident and secure in the work and service that lies ahead.

Motivation and Commitment

This is also a community-building ministry. When a group of acolytes forms, esprit de corps grows as the team works together, through fellowship activities and through the acolytes' pride in being part of an elite—although not exclusive—guild.

> Developing a sense of community helps keep acolytes committed to the ministry of serving, and encourages their continuing involvement as they move into their later teens.

A way to foster development of the community is to form pairs or teams of acolytes at different skill levels, who work together for several months and then are regrouped with other peers. Not only do they learn from each other, but also friendships are formed and grow. Developing a sense of community helps keep acolytes committed to the ministry of serving, and in the case of adolescent acolytes, encourages their continuing involvement as they move into their later teens.

Be sure to include the measurement of the acolytes' skill levels as part of the ongoing training program, and to celebrate their accomplishments and commitment to the ministry. You can recognize levels of excellence by using special crosses or medals, various ribbon colors, differing vestments, and other signs as acolytes progress from novice to experienced levels. Or describe different stages of progress symbolically by using words particularly appropriate to your parish, such as the narthex, nave, or chancel teams.

Worship as a Part of Training

It is important to include a worship experience at the beginning of every training session to help participants and leaders become spiritually centered and focused on their work in the Lord's service. Build variety into the training program by using the various liturgies found in *The Book of Common Prayer* (BCP). This practice also will give acolytes an opportunity to experience the liturgical richness found in the Prayer Book. An additional benefit to varying the services is that different lay and ordained ministers will be involved in the services, which will help develop rapport between the acolytes and the leaders they will assist.

One challenge in working with acolytes is that clergy come and go. Every time there is a change in personnel, the expectations and duties for acolytes tend to change, too. However, the basics don't change: If there are candles, acolytes light them; if there is a processional cross, an acolyte carries it. But it's the way the candles are lit, and where and how the cross is carried that vary. It's easy to visualize seasoned acolytes shaking their heads and saying, "Here comes a new priest (read "new way of doing things")!"

Training Theory

The goal of training is to help acolytes retain information that is important, to help them do their jobs, and, even more important, to understand and internalize the significance of their ministry. To that end, we suggest developing a training program built around the workshops in this book. Combining group activities, one-on-one training, and lots of peer interaction, these exercises will encourage acolytes to:

- pay attention to the material being presented;

- think about what they are doing and why they are doing it;

- observe what is going on in liturgies and the acolytes' roles in them

- relate to one another and build a solid community that is centered around service.

Workshop training—like all good teaching—is most effective if it has **three characteristics:**

- a flexible plan;
- regular repetition of key points;
- full participation of all members of the group.

There will be, of course, distractions. Attendance will not always meet your expectations, and the inevitable changes that take place when clergy or acolytes come to or leave a parish can be unsettling and confusing; however, by accepting these realities as a part of life, you will find that the program still works.

The need for flexibility, sometimes described as "spontaneous creativity," can be threatening to leaders. It is, however, an essential ingredient when working with young people as you try to foster their interest in understanding and working within the complicated and often uneven traditions of the Church. Your responsiveness to their learning patterns—your flexibility—will reflect your interest in their journey—and indeed will reflect your own youth.

Flexibility in the workshops also is important because acolytes in one parish may well represent a variety of church backgrounds. That diversity would certainly be evident in diocesan workshops. What may be a basic responsibility, practice, or understanding in one congregation may be optional or even unheard of in another.

Repetition of basic principles must be a part of every training experience and should not be neglected, regardless of the acolytes' experience or expertise. In workshops and small groups, the acolytes' growth in their understanding of common denominators such as candles, offering plates, and processional crosses should be identified and recognized. At the same time their understanding should be challenged by representing these basic concepts from different perspectives. We suggest techniques that can be used to make the necessary repetition of basic principles more interesting and engaging.

In each workshop participation of acolytes at all levels of experience is strongly encouraged. Workshops should be designed so beginners learn from experienced acolytes, and those who "know the ropes" have the opportunity to train beginners. Constant interaction among experience levels gives acolytes opportunities to learn nuances of their ministry that trainers might not think to offer.

Once upon a time, during an acolyte festival a young acolyte mentioned the "Sunday School Cross." When asked what that was, she explained that it was the cross the acolyte uses to lead the Sunday school students into the church at the Peace. Many heads nodded in understanding as she explained how the procession worked, while other people were surprised. Proving that good ideas spread, after the festival at least one parish decided to adopt the Sunday School Cross as part of its tradition.

Training "Nuts and Bolts"

The Training Team

You are the best judge of the resources that you will need and that will be available to carry out two important aspects of the training job:

- conveying information about the tasks to be done and the way to do them, and
- encouraging the growing acolyte community.

A clergyperson and an acolyte director would be the ideal primary team, with the director carrying the planning and organizing burden. However, have as many additional people as possible involved on the extended training team to provide a variety of perspectives on the ministry. For example, an altar guild member, an experienced or even a former acolyte, or a seminarian could play an important role. Occasional visits by clergy from other parishes would provide a different and broadening point of view.

TRAINING RESOURCES

- ALTAR GUILD
- SEMINARIANS DOING FIELD WORK
- CLERGY FROM SURROUNDING AREA
- ACOLYTES FROM OTHER PARISHES

Schedule Options

A variety of workshop experiences will deepen the acolytes' understanding of their roles and responsibilities. Depending on available time, personal schedules, the size of the group, segments of the series that follows could be used one at a time (say, one every two weeks), or several could be grouped together for a longer session. The key to developing an effective training schedule is that the pattern be cyclical. The workshops, in whatever order, should be repeated annually—bi-annually if possible—to hone skills of current acolytes and to bring new acolytes into the fold.

Timing suggestions for each workshop are simply that—suggestions to help you plan. Feel free to vary them according to your schedule and your observations about how the group functions. We do recommend a minimum of 45 minutes for worship to allow time for preparation and reflection on the experience.

Worried? Don't be.
You have a desire to maintain and extend the traditions of the Church; and, you believe in young people and their ability to be an important avenue to carry on those traditions.

So,
when the situation calls for flexibility—and perhaps creativity—take a measure of the tradition you want to teach, then add a healthy dose of the youth in your own heart, and you'll come out fine.

Materials and Space

For each workshop, have available the following materials:

✔ newsprint

✔ easel and markers

✔ blackboard and chalk
  or wipe-off board and dry markers

✔ copy of *The Book of
  Common Prayer* for everyone

✔ acolyte manual
  (see Resources in the Appendices)

✔ copy of the Glossary
  (see the Appendices)

✔ *Dictionary of the Christian Church*
  for every participant

Depending on which workshop is being used, space requirements should be assessed and space reserved. Arrangements should be made to use the worship space or another area that can be adapted for worship. From time to time, having access to the sacristy might be helpful.

WORKSHOPS FOR ACOLYTES

The Workshop Approach

The workshops that follow are divided into five sections:

- ■ **Introduction to Ministry**

- ■ **Introduction to Liturgies**

- ■ **Focus on Beginning Acolytes**

- ■ **Focus on Intermediate Acolytes**

- ■ **Focus on Advanced Acolytes**

Even though some workshops are designed to meet the needs of certain experience levels, exercises in all the workshops can be used either with a group of acolytes with the same experience level, or with a mixed group. Leaders should decide which approach to use; both models work. If there are enough acolytes and trainers to have groups of acolytes at the same level, they can move smoothly through the workshops, which deepen in complexity. As mentioned earlier, though, there are advantages for working with the whole group. For example, repetition of basic information might be helpful reinforcement for more experienced acolytes. While concepts in the advanced sections might be simply informational for beginning acolytes, exposure to the ideas will provide a preliminary foundation for the time when the acolytes delve into the material more deeply in future training sessions. Another argument for blended groups is that they provide opportunities for experienced acolytes to assume an apprentice–leader role. A compromise approach might be to vary the composition of the groups within the training cycle.

Regardless of which model is being used, it is important to allow adequate time to cover the material and to give the acolytes ample opportunity to ask questions and be comfortable with the concepts. Again, any number of exercises can be used in each workshop, depending on available time.

The Pattern for Each Workshop:

I. Worship
using a variety of service forms;
see next page for suggestions.

II. Introduction of concepts
including:
- the role of the acolyte
- acolytes' personal goals
- needs of the parish
- service elements

III. Group exercises
emphasizing at least one of the following:
- definitions
- basic points
- functions and flow
- special occasions
- leadership roles for acolytes
- testing

IV. Conclusion
reflection and feedback;
see page 18 for additional
information.

The Beginning and End of Each Workshop

The theological bookends of each workshop session should be worship at the beginning, as discussed earlier, and a clear conclusion, a regathering of the group for brief prayer and reflection at the end of the workshop.

Alpha: Worship

(45 minutes+)

In addition to being an appropriate way to begin training for service in the Church, acolyte worship services will give participants an opportunity to observe and assume a variety of roles within the services. We suggest that a minimum of 45 minutes be allowed at the beginning of each workshop for worship.

The more familiar acolytes are with a variety of liturgies, the easier it will be for them to adapt from one to another and to work with clergy whose styles differ. In a sense, the worship experience in itself is training. Although today the majority of Episcopal congregations celebrate the Eucharist every Sunday, some occasionally schedule Morning Prayer services, and Baptisms are scheduled either alone or in conjunction with the Eucharist. Comfort with both rites of Holy Eucharist will stand acolytes in good stead for whatever comes their way. If time allows for a brief homily or meditation, it would be an ideal time to raise issues related to servant ministry.

If you are not using the church or chapel, have the workshop worship space clearly defined and prepared with an altar, the elements, seats, music, prayer books. The space should be configured as closely as possible to the worship space in which the acolytes will serve. In advance of the service, give liturgical assignments to participants—clergy, readers, acolytes, liturgical assistants, musicians, and so on. Make preparations for work that should be done when the service has concluded.

At an Acolyte Festival a group of servers who had never worked together were asked to serve as a team for the closing Eucharist. More than a hundred of their peers were in attendance, and they had only an hour to prepare. Panic! But, they were guided in their planning by the Head Acolyte from the Cathedral, whose experience and leadership paid off. The service went smoothly and the acolytes felt a great sense of accomplishment.

Omega: Conclusion

(10 minutes +/-)

To bring an orderly end to the workshop, a concluding exercise of about 10 minutes should be offered to provide an opportunity for reflection on the experience and feedback.

The theological reason for this segment is to give the participants and trainers time to give thanks to God for bringing the acolyte servant ministry into their lives and for the understanding and relationships that come with it. Beyond that, participants may well have observations and final questions and may have comments about the experience. It also might be a time for the workshop leader or leaders to comment on the progress they have observed. The length of time taken to conclude the workshop is not as important as simply providing the closing moment.

FIVE WORKSHOPS

A. Introduction to the Acolyte Ministry

B. Introduction to Liturgies

C. For New Acolytes

D. For Intermediate Acolytes

E. For Advanced Acolytes

Workshop A:
Introduction to the Acolyte Ministry

Goal:
Link "definition" of an acolyte and each acolyte's personal goals

Objectives:
Explore the history and meaning of the ministry; explore the acolytes' role

I. Worship (45 minutes)

II. Introduction of Concepts
Being an acolyte is a valid way of serving the Church. Lay ministers, both young and old, often have a difficult time conceiving of their Sunday morning time in vestments as anything more than filling a hole. As a result, they don't see much wider value in acolyting.

In this first exercise, then, they will learn that the core value of ministry is to serve, that serving has always been the Church's given mission of the acolyte, and that serving in this capacity has an integrity of its own.

III. Exercises
Exercise 1:

What is an acolyte? (20 minutes)

On newsprint or blackboard, make three columns with the following headings:

• "Acolyte" in the center
• BCP page 365 (reference to ministers in the Eucharist)
• BCP page 855 (Who are the ministers in the Church?—catechism)

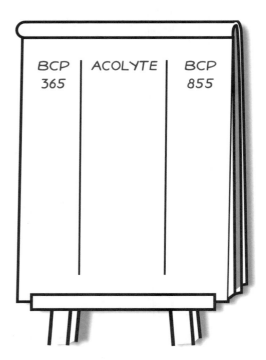

BCP 365	ACOLYTE	BCP 855

 Ask: What is an acolyte?

 Record answers under "Acolyte."

Ask participants to look on the two prayer book pages to see if they can find a reference to acolytes.

• Point out all references to "ministers." Record answers under appropriate page reference. (Refer to the *Dictionary of the Christian Church*. Note historical mention of ordained acolytes.)

- Point out the importance of lay acolyte ministry.
- We are ministers by virtue of our Baptism. (Everyone is called to ministry in Baptism; that ministry is exercised through one's calling as an acolyte.)

 Record new ideas in the "Acolyte" column.

For example:
- special ministers
- people trained to serve Christ

Go back to first question.
Push for other definitions—leading to "minister."

 Ask: What does a minister do?

 Record responses.
Look for "serve" as an answer.
Explore uses of word "service."

For example:
- doing service in the church
- church service

Explain that *server* and *acolyte* are interchangeable words. Refer to glossary for definitions.

Exercise 2:
How do acolytes serve?
(15 minutes)

Explore what members of the group have seen acolytes do in worship services.

Brainstorm other ways that acolytes serve.

Possibilities:
- lighting the Paschal Candle, altar candles
- extinguishing the candles
- holding the baptismal candle
- assisting the priest at Baptisms
- moving Gospel book on altar
- ushering during communion
- leading the Sunday School procession
- assisting with the offering plates
- participating in the Gospel procession
- carrying Gospel book
- processional cross, torches, incense
- assisting with the elements, lavabo
- acting as crucifer
- banner-bearer
- flag-bearer, torch-bearer
- closing altar rail gates
- other activities as mentioned

Return to duties in Catechism (BCP, pg 855) to illuminate additional responsibilities.

Exercise 3:
Whom do you serve?
(10 minutes)

 Ask: When you serve as an acolyte (citing listed duties), whom are you serving?

 Record responses.

Look for the following answers:

    Serve the Lord

    Serve the priest

    Serve the Lord by serving the priest

    Serve the people of the congregation

Exercise 4:
Acolytes' personal goals
(40 minutes)

If time is an issue, this could be used as a separate workshop after Introduction to Liturgies workshop.

Break into small groups to discuss how the definitions and responsibilities discussed earlier fit with each person's interests, skills, and goals. Facilitators of the groups should be trainers, adult or experienced acolytes.

Come back together and talk about common points that were mentioned in the small group discussion.

IV. Conclusion
(10 minutes)

Refer to page 18 for concluding activities.

Workshop B
Introduction to Liturgies

Goal:
Familiarize acolytes with various worship services

Objective:
Using the BCP, analyze primary then secondary services

I. Worship (45 minutes)

II. Introduction of Concepts
Based on the worship experience at the beginning of the session, this exercise draws on the acolytes' powers of observation and recall.

It will help familiarize acolytes with the service and make them comfortable with its movement. As they experience more worship forms, they will help discover commonalities and patterns that are consistent in all services.

III. Exercises
Exercise 1:
Explore services used during worship. (60 minutes)

 Ask: the group to recall the "pieces" of the worship service they just experienced.

 List them on newsprint.

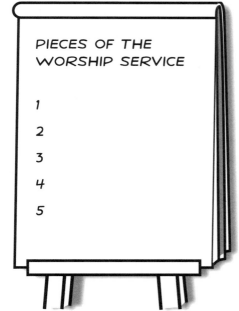

PIECES OF THE
WORSHIP SERVICE

1

2

3

4

5

Invite the group to look through the pages of the BCP containing that worship service.

For example:
- Holy Eucharist Rite II

Ask them to identify elements of the service.

Suggest looking at headings of various sizes.

Look also at Rubrics—clues often printed in red —that give very specific directions about how to proceed, and why.

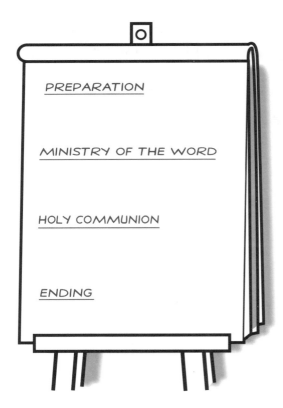

Add those elements to the first list. Solicit observations until a complete list has been drawn.

Write the following words on newsprint leaving space under each:

> preparation
> ministry of the Word
> Holy Communion
> ending

Review the list that the group prepared. Insert service elements into the correct categories.

Exercise 2:
Continue to Explore Services
(45 minutes)

Do the same exercise using another service.

For example:
■ Morning Prayer if the Eucharist was studied first.

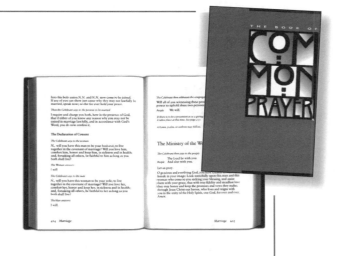

Explore other services as time allows, or repeat the exercise using other services in future training sessions. Note the blending of services described in the rubrics. For instance, in the BCP pp. 310–311, there are alternatives within the service of Holy Baptism. Discuss how these alternatives may effect acolyte responsibilities.

IV. Conclusion
(10 minutes)

Refer to page 18 for concluding activities.

Workshop C
For New Acolytes

Goal:
Acquaint acolytes with basics of serving

Objective:
Intellectually work through concepts related to serving and objects used

I. Worship (45 minutes)

II. Introduction of Concepts

This workshop is designed to teach acolytes what they are holding, where to go, where to stand, how to stand, what to do, and—of equal importance—how to stay focused on the service and on their responsibilities. The exercises will help each acolyte to do his or her job with confidence.

III. Exercises

Exercise 1:

Understanding Concepts
(30 minutes)

Prepare a list of concepts with which acolytes should be familiar.

- ■ Acclamation
- ■ Seasons of the church year
- ■ Ascension
- ■ Benediction

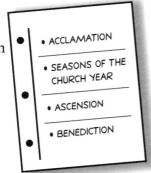

- • ACCLAMATION
- • SEASONS OF THE CHURCH YEAR
- • ASCENSION
- • BENEDICTION

Give each person in the group a number, at random, as identification.

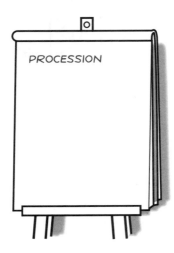

PROCESSION

Write one word from list of concepts on newsprint.

Ask Acolyte #1 to read the word and then define it. If the acolyte is unable to describe the concept, write another word (perhaps a more obvious concept, like "procession") and give him or her another opportunity to describe it.

Continue listing words until the first acolyte has made a correct identification.

Move to Acolyte #2, and give him or her the opportunity to describe a word that the first acolyte didn't know.

Continue the process around the room until all the words on the list have been considered.

Exercise 2:
Understanding Objects
(30 minutes)

Use the same process to identify objects used in worship services. The name of the object could be written, a drawing or photo used, or the object itself could be displayed.

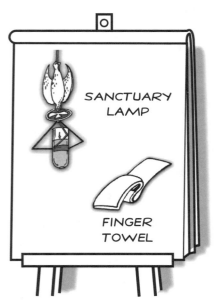

SANCTUARY LAMP

FINGER TOWEL

If a visual approach is used write the name on newsprint when it has been identified to make verbal connection—to help the acolytes remember the term as well as the object's appearance.

If the group is a combination of more and less experienced acolytes, including some more arcane concepts or objects adds some interest for those who have been serving for a longer time, and might be intriguing for new acolytes.

Exercise 3:
Understanding Functions and Duties
(30 minutes)

Prepare a list of typical acolyte duties and functions.

Invite an experienced acolyte to choose an item from the list, such as carrying the cross or flag, and walk through (mime) the process without using props. The group's task is to identify what is being done. Give a token "prize" for the first correct answer.

Continue the process, using other duties and functions on the list, as time allows.

Exercise 4:
Practicing Functions and Duties
(30 minutes)

Have a newer acolyte act out one of the functions or duties on the prepared list.

Ask a more experienced acolyte to offer a positive critique after the mimed action is complete. Include comments about posture and stance.

Give the "mime" acolytes an opportunity to repeat the action until they feel comfortable to with what they are being asked to do.

IV. Conclusion
(10 minutes)

Refer to page 18 for concluding activities.

Workshop D
For Intermediate Acolytes

Goal:
Provide more in-depth understanding of worship services

Objective:
Explore how and why parts of worship services work together

I. Worship (45 minutes)

II. Introduction of Concepts
The focus of these exercises should be beyond the basics, helping acolytes understand how to apply them. Beginning acolytes should be encouraged to participate as they can. Count on—press for—more experienced members of the group to delve for answers.

III. Exercises
Exercise 1:
Review Objects
(20 minutes)

Develop a scavenger hunt, using a series of clues that will take the acolytes to five (or so) places where they will find or be reminded of several objects that you want to review. The group can be broken into two teams; each team will have separate clues with one final goal. Have a small prize for both teams at the end of the hunt.

For example:

Clue #1:   Go to the place where the Reserved Sacrament is held during the week.
(Aumbry)

Clue #2:   Your next clue will be found where people place their material gifts made in thanksgiving to God.
(Alms Basin)

Clue # 3:   Your next clue will be found where the bread is kept before it is consecrated.
(Ciborium)

Clue #4:   Your next clue will be found on that object that the crucifer carries.
(Processional cross)

The same game could be used to focus on functions; clues could be related to specific places acolytes stand or sit or assist during worship services.

Exercise 2:
Outline Flow of Worship Service
(30–45 minutes)

Invite the members of the group, drawing on memory and using the prayer book as a resource, to note and record on newsprint all parts of the service, and the acolytes' responsibility at each point.

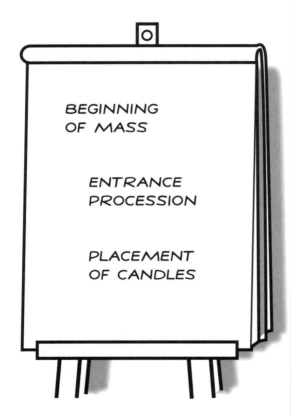

BEGINNING
OF MASS

ENTRANCE
PROCESSION

PLACEMENT
OF CANDLES

Suggest that they begin the list with their own preparation, including:

- the time they should arrive at the church

- vesting

- reading the order of service

- then move to the gathering

- procession, and so on.

(In a diocesan workshop, it is interesting to note the variety of service elements.)

Exercise 3:
Study Flow of Worship Services
(30 minutes)

Pair intermediate acolytes with a more experienced or adult member of the group. Ask the less experienced member to read through a service aloud, describing each acolyte function along the way. Ask the more senior member to listen for missed points and elaborate on them.

Exercise 4:
Experience Flow of Worship Services
(45 minutes)

In the worship space, have the intermediate group walk through an entire service, describing what they are doing at each point. Ask the experienced acolytes to function as observers, noting points that could stand correction.

When the "service" is complete, ask the acolytes to talk about why various things are done in the worship service (e.g., processing, reverencing, standing, kneeling, and so on), reasons for the sequence of actions, and how the parts of the service fit together.

This exercise could be repeated several times, using a variety of services.

IV. Conclusion
(10 minutes)
Refer to page 18 for concludinig activities.

Workshop E
For Advanced Acolytes

Goal:

Prepare acolytes for further service

Objectives:

Develop skills as apprentice trainers. Develop ability to anticipate expectations of clergy and other participants' needs in special service situations.

I. Worship (45 minutes)

II. Introduction of Concepts

The role of experienced acolytes is twofold: To be perceived as leaders in the acolyte group, and to be available when they are needed to provide special service on such occasions as ordinations, festival days, and Bishops' visits. Some determination should be made about when an acolyte has achieved this level—the number of years of service is the most likely marker. This group might be set apart using a special designation such as Senior Acolyte, Bishop's Acolyte, or Head Server.

Adult acolytes deserve special mention here. Some will have been acolytes for many years and therefore fall into the normal "experienced" category. Some, however, will have only recently discerned this as a new ministry. Even if they have been church members for many years, they will benefit by learning basic concepts along with the younger acolytes. However, you can also take advantage of their maturity.

Take and ask them to function, when appropriate, as assistant trainers, along with the younger experienced acolytes.

III. Exercises
Exercise 1:
Review
(30 minutes)

Ask one acolyte to conduct a guided tour of the sacristy and vesting room for new and intermediate acolytes.

Ask a member of the altar guild to talk about the provenance of each object used during the service and how it is cared for.

Ask a member of the clergy to discuss the history and meaning of each of the vestments commonly used and how it is cared for.

Once a year the trainer should meet individually with experienced acolytes to discuss and affirm their growth and development. Ask them to commit to continuing their advanced service as acolytes by assisting in the training of their less experienced peers.

Exercise 2:
Leadership Experience
(60 minutes +)

Ask each acolyte to:

- design an introductory exercise for beginners

- lead the exercise

- conduct a group evaluation of the exercise.

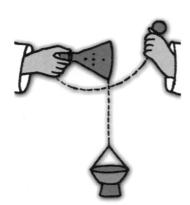

Exercise 3:
Anticipation Skills—Written Tests
(40 minutes)

Write several liturgical scenarios (*see examples*) on a sheet of paper, leaving a blank space between each of them. Distribute the sheets to the group. Ask them to describe, in writing, the next acolyte duty required for each. Have them exchange their answers with another acolyte for corrections.

Discuss questions, differences.

Examples:
The Celebrant or Deacon returns the bread box and cruets to the server after preparing the elements on the altar. What should the server be anticipating?

The lavabo.

The Passing of the Peace is taking place, and the acolyte notices that the Offering Plates are missing. What should s/he do?

Anticipating the Offertory, the acolyte goes to the sacristy, retrieves the Offering Plates and returns to the Chancel, prepared to pass them to the Ushers.

Exercise 4:
Anticipation Skills
(30 minutes)

Give each participant a tablet and pen.

Describe a liturgical scenario, verbally or dramatically.

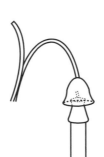

Have each participant describe in writing what should happen next—without saying anything aloud. When everyone is ready, go around the room and have each person read his or her answer aloud. Discuss questions, differences.

Exercise 5:
Special Services, Festival Days
(60 minutes)

Using *The Book of Common Prayer*, choose a special service such as Ordination, Easter Vigil, or Celebration and Blessing of a Marriage. Read through the liturgy, then make assignments for each participant and walk through the service (much like a wedding rehearsal). Conclude with observations (offered by the trainer and peers), questions, and clarification where necessary.

IV. Conclusion
(10 minutes)
Refer to page 18 for concluding activities.

APPENDICES

In the appendices you will find:

- ■ A brief reflective service that is recommended for acolytes, to be used before they serve

- ■ Several prayers recommended for acolytes or trainers

- ■ An outline of acolytes' typical responsibilities before and after a worship service

- ■ A list of resources for trainers

- ■ A glossary

Prayerful Preparation

Personal, prayerful preparation *to be used by*
acolytes before the liturgy

In the Exhortation before the service of the Holy
Eucharist in the BCP, p. 316, we are told that "if
we are to share rightly in the celebration of those
Holy Mysteries, and be nourished by that spiritual
Food [the Body and Blood of our Lord Jesus
Christ], we must remember the dignity of that
Holy Sacrament." Careful preparation should be
made then before receiving the Sacrament.
St. Paul said it this way:

> A [person] ought to examine himself before he
> eats of the bread and drinks of the cup. For
> anyone who eats and drinks without recognizing
> the body of the Lord eats and drinks judgment
> on himself.
>
> *(First Corinthians 11:28-29,*
> *New International Version)*

Our Eucharistic liturgy is designed so that anyone
who actively participates in it will have done this
preparation of recognizing the body and blood of
our Lord Jesus. However, the greatest benefit comes
from self-examination before arriving at the
service.

1. Relax in a place away from the noise and
   normal distractions of your world. Find a quiet
   place, kneel or sit, and begin to be aware of
   God's presence. God is ever-present,
   surrounding us with divine love and mercy. Try
   repeating several times: "Jesus, you are present
   with me. Thank you." Our God is forever
   willing to receive us, even when we seem to

turn our back on God. Renew your willingness
to follow the Son of God, Jesus Christ, the
Risen One, as your Lord and King.

2. Read the Gospel lesson for the next Sunday. The
   reading can be found in the lectionary of the
   BCP for Year A, B, or C (see instructions on p.
   888). Identify one idea or phrase in the lesson
   that has particular meaning for you. Reflect on
   this for a few minutes.

3. Confess your sins, considering your life this
   past week with God, yourself, your family,
   friends and neighbors.

   > *O Lord, in your presence, I confess I have*
   > *_____ .*
   > *I am truly sorry, and I repent and turn to you for*
   > *forgiveness, in the Name of Jesus Christ. Amen.*

4. Receive God's forgiveness by faith, knowing
   that God's promise of forgiveness is for those
   who, in true repentance and faith in Jesus
   Christ, confess their sins, recognizing their
   dependence upon the Lord.

   > *Thank you, Lord, for forgiving me. I receive*
   > *your forgiveness by faith, in the Name of*
   > *Jesus Christ. Amen.*

5. Close in prayer:

   > *Help me, Lord, to present myself as a living*
   > *sacrifice to you, that I may serve you and*
   > *your Church faithfully, and worthily receive*
   > *the Body and Blood of Christ. Amen.*

Recite the Lord's Prayer.

Additional Prayers

At any time:

O God, you have angels who stand in front of your throne to serve you day and night; I ask you to bless with your Holy Spirit the acolytes of your Church, that serving in front and around your earthly throne they may do so with reverence and true holiness, to the honor and glory of your Name; through your Son, Jesus Christ our Lord. Amen.

Just before a service:

Lord Jesus, I give you thanks for letting me serve you in your Church today. Help me to keep my thoughts on you as I do my various duties in the sanctuary. Bless all those who minister today and all those who have come to worship. I pray that what I do in service may be your will for me. In the power of your Name I pray. Amen.

Just before receiving Communion:

Be present, be present, O Jesus, our great High Priest, as you were present with your disciples, and be known to us in the breaking of bread.

Responsibilities Before and After the Service

Personal appearance

A seemingly obvious point that might need reinforcement is that the acolytes' appearance really does make a difference. It is a distraction to worshippers when acolytes haven't paid careful attention to the condition of their hair, hands, and fingernails, or to their shoes and the clothing they wear under vestments.

Vestments

The most important of the acolytes' responsibilities for their vestments is to be sure they are clean and in good condition; the Acolyte Director's role is to have a plan in place to care for the vestments. A member of the Altar Guild, an acolyte parent volunteer, a sexton, or the acolyte and/or his/her parent(s) should be prepared to clean, repair, and press vestments whenever necessary. Acolytes should examine their vestments after each service to see what is needed and should make arrangements to have them returned in time for the next service.

Schedule

A service assignment schedule should be posted in the room where acolytes vest, and acolytes should be encouraged to check it every week, whether or not they are serving, to be sure of their own assignments and to note any service changes. Each acolyte should be in communication with the director if an assignment change is necessary.

Nave, Sanctuary

Although in most parishes the altar guild and sexton are responsible for ensuring that the nave and sanctuary are orderly and clean after each service, acolytes should take some responsibility for offering assistance. Even if they are not primarily responsible, they should have a thorough understanding of where things are kept and how they are handled, in case their services are needed.

Resources

These manuals provide helpful hints on basic acolyte principles:

A Manual for Acolytes, by Dennis G. Michno. Morehouse Publishing, 1981. (particularly helpful for Episcopalians)

The New Complete Server, by Christopher Heller. Morehouse Publishing, 1995.

Other published resources:

Oxford Dictionary of the Christian Church, edited by F. L. Cross, Oxford University Press, 1958.

Events:

The National Acolyte Festival, held every fall at the Washington National Cathedral in Washington, D.C.

For more information

contact the Festival Convener:
John Ball
P.O. Box 207
St. Mary's City, MD 20686
Phone: (301) 862-4597
Fax: (301) 862-2507
Email: trinitysmcmd@olg.com

Check with your diocesan office about diocesan or provincial acolyte training or festivals.

GLOSSARY

Note: Words and definitions are apt to differ between churches and denominations. Capitalized words within a definition are also defined in this glossary.

ACOLYTE

One who assists the ordained and licensed ministers at worship services. *The Oxford Dictionary of the Christian Church* says, "The duties of the acolyte are to light the altar candles, to carry the candles in procession, to prepare the wine and water for the Mass, and to assist the Sacred Ministers at Mass." Synonyms include Servers, altar boys, altar girls.

ALB

A white, sleeved garment, reaching to the ankles, worn as a Eucharistic vestment. It is sometimes hooded, or worn with an Amice, which is a wide linen "collar."

ALMS BASIN

The large, usually silver, brass, or wood plate that is used to hold the smaller Offering Plates. Technically, an alms basin and an offering plate are the same.

ALTAR

Sometimes called "the Lord's Table," the altar is the large wood or stone table located in a central part of the Sanctuary. It is the focal point of any liturgical Church, the place where Holy Communion is celebrated.

ALTAR CANDLES

Candles that are usually placed on each end of the altar. In many churches, these are a symbol that the liturgy of the Holy Eucharist is to be celebrated.

ALTAR RAIL

The rail or cushions where Episcopalians traditionally come to receive Holy Communion. In some churches it serves as a dividing line, within the Chancel, between the Choir and the Sanctuary.

ALTAR RAIL GATE

A gate in the Altar Rail that, when open, provides access to the Altar area and is closed during administration of Holy Communion, provides a continuous Altar Rail.

AMICE

A square or rectangular white cloth worn under the alb as a hood or over the shoulders. It is held in place by strings that are wound around the neck then tied around the chest and waist.

AUMBRY

The lockable cupboard, often on the wall or built into the wall of the Sanctuary, where the Reserved Sacrament and Holy Oils are kept. (See Tabernacle.)

BANNER

A large, colorfully designed cloth often attached to a wooden pole, carried in procession, and displayed in the Chancel or Nave. Banners usually depict symbols of the Christian faith, including that of the congregation itself.

BANNER BEARER

The Acolyte who is responsible for a banner in procession.

BREAD BOX

A small silver or gold, round or square box that holds the Wafers (bread) used for Holy Communion. (See Ciborium.)

BURSE

A flat, square, lined or silk case (or purse) that holds the Corporal and Purificators. It sits on the Chalice, over the Chalice Veil, before and after Holy Communion.

CANDELABRA

A multi-branch candle stand that typically holds 3 to 7 candles. One or more can be used, free-standing or on a Retable, but rarely on the Altar. These candles are used in addition to Altar Candles on feast days (like Christmas or Easter). They are sometimes used alone, without the Altar Candles, for Morning or Evening Prayer. (See Office Lights.)

CANDLE LIGHTER

A metal and wood pole containing a Taper or liquid wax device that is used to light Altar Candles or Candelabra. It has a "snuffer," used to extinguish lit candles.

CASSOCK

An ankle-length garment worn under the Alb, Surplice, or Cotta. The usual color for Clergy is black, although bishops and cathedral clergy traditionally wear purple. It is worn under a Surplice for Morning and Evening Prayer and other Pastoral Offices.

CASSOCK-ALB

A white, sleeved, double-breasted garment, reaching to the ankles. It was originally developed to be worn by Clergy instead of a Cassock and an Alb during Holy Eucharist services. It is now also being worn by any lay or ordained minister, including Acolytes and choir members, at any service.

CELEBRANT

The priest or bishop who leads the celebration of, or presides at, the Holy Eucharist. (See Officiant.)

CHALICE

A cup or goblet made of silver or gold, or of wood, pottery, glass, etc., used to hold wine for the consecration and administration of the Blood of Christ during Holy Communion.

CHALICE BEARER

A Eucharistic assistant who is licensed by the bishop to administer the wine during Holy Communion.

CHALICE VEIL

A large fabric square, usually silk, placed over the Chalice and Paten before and after Holy Communion. Its color usually symbolizes the current church season or feast day.

CHANCEL

The part of the Church east of the Nave. It includes the Sanctuary and the Choir. In some church buildings, a large beam or a wrought iron fence, called the Rood Beam or Screen, marks the separation of these two main areas. Most churches at least have steps at this juncture.

CHASUBLE

An oval, poncho-like garment worn by the Celebrant over the Alb.

CHOIR

The part of the Church where the members of the choir sit. In traditional architecture it is the westerly section of the Chancel, and also is the area where the Officiants' Prayer Desks are set for leading Morning and Evening Prayer.

CHRISTUS REX

Latin for "Christ the King." A Crucifix including an image of Christ wearing a crown or halo and a royal robe, without any nails. It represents the victory of the Risen Christ over death, and his resulting kingship.

CHURCH (Capital 'C')

"...the Body of which Jesus Christ is head, and of which all baptized persons are members" (BCP, p. 854). The capitalized word also is used to describe a congregation or a denomination as a whole, e.g. the Episcopal Church.

CHURCH (Lower-case 'c')

The term used to designate a building designed for the purpose of worshiping God.

CIBORIUM

A Bread Box in the shape of a Chalice, usually with a lid.

CINCTURE

A flat cloth, or rope Girdle, worn around the waist to hold the Cassock or Alb in place.

CLERGY

Deacons, priests, and bishops of the Church. For their specific functions, see pp. 855-856 of the BCP.

CLERGY CRUCIFER

The Acolyte who carries the processional cross immediately before the Clergy.

COMMUNICANT

One who receives or is entitled to receive Holy Communion.

COPE

A cape or cloak worn by the Clergy in procession and on special occasions.

CORPORAL

A square piece of white linen spread on the altar during preparation of the Elements for Holy Communion, and upon which is placed the Chalice and Paten.

COTTA

A short white garment worn by Acolytes over the Cassock. (See Surplice.)

CREDENCE TABLE

A small table, either free-standing or built into the wall, usually on the Epistle side of the Sanctuary, upon which the Cruets, Bread Box, and Lavabo are placed.

CRUCIFER

An Acolyte who carries a processional cross.

CRUCIFIX

Any cross upon which is a figure of the crucified Jesus. (See Christus Rex.)

CRUETS

Bottles or pitchers that hold the wine and water for the Holy Communion.

DIOCESE

A geographical area of the Church, containing a certain number of Parishes and Missions. Spiritual and administrative leaders of dioceses are Bishops, elected by the Clergy of the diocese and elected deputies from each congregation.

ELEMENTS

Physical, outward signs of sacraments. Bread and Wine are elements of the Holy Eucharist; Water is the element of Baptism.

EPISTLE

A Bible reading from one of the New Testament Letters, the Acts of the Apostles, or the Book of Revelation, read before the Gospel in the Holy Eucharist service. The word "epistle" comes from the Greek word "letter." The Epistle is usually read from the Lectern.

EPISTLE SIDE

Facing the Altar, this side is to the right, the side from which, in older liturgical traditions, the Epistle was read.

EUCHARIST

A synonym for the service of Holy Communion. It comes from a Greek word meaning "thanksgiving."

FLAGBEARER

The Acolyte who carries a flag in procession.

FONT

Any receptacle used to hold the water of Holy Baptism. In most Episcopal churches the Font is a bowl on a stand or table, but it may also refer to a larger baptistry for baptism by total immersion.

FUNERAL PALL

The full-length cloth that covers the casket at a funeral service.

GENUFLECT

A reverential action in which one momentarily kneels on the right knee, normally done only when the Reserved Sacrament is present in a Church. (See Reverence.)

GIRDLE

A rope, usually of white or black cotton, tied around the waist to hold the Alb or Cassock in place. (See Cincture.)

GOSPEL

The final lesson during the Ministry of the Word in a Holy Eucharist service, taken from one of the four Gospels of the New Testament. During the service the Gospel is read only by a deacon or priest. The congregation stands while the Gospel is read to honor the life and Good News of Jesus Christ. The Gospel is proclaimed from the center of the Chancel or, after procession, the Nave.

GOSPEL SIDE

Facing the Altar, this is the side to the left, from which, in older liturgical traditions, the Gospel was read.

HEAD CRUCIFER

The Acolyte who carries a processional cross at the head (beginning) of a procession.

HOLY OILS

Oils consecrated by a bishop. The Oil of Chrism is used typically at Baptisms, Confirmations and Ordinations, and for other special blessings; the Oil for Healing (or Oil of the Sick) is used during healing services.

HOST

The bread, after it has been consecrated, in the Eucharist. The larger wafer, the "Priest's Host" is used by the Celebrant. (See Wafer.)

INCENSE

A mixture of gums and spices, which, when burned, provides an aromatic smoke for liturgical use. The rising incense smoke symbolizes our rising prayers to God. (See Revelation 5:8.)

LAITY

From the Greek word laos, it broadly means "the People of God." The word is normally used to distinguish members of the Church from the ordained ministers.

LAVABO

A bowl used by the celebrant in which to wash his or her hands after the Offertory during the Holy Eucharist preparation of the Elements, or other times such as when oil or chrism is used, or after the imposition of ashes on Ash Wednesday. The hands are dried using a Lavabo Towel.

LAVABO TOWEL

A rectangular white linen towel used by the celebrant to dry his or her hands after water is poured over them above the Lavabo.

LAY READER

A member of the laity licensed by the bishop to read the lessons, conduct certain services in the absence of a deacon or priest, and, if specially licensed, to administer the Chalice at Holy Communion. (See Chalice Bearer.)

LECTERN

The large wooden or metal stand, usually on the Epistle Side, from which the Scripture lessons are read.

LECTOR

A person licensed to read a lesson during a worship service.

LINENS

Delicate, white cloths used in the Sanctuary to cover the Altar, and as towels.

MISSAL

A book used on the Altar by the Celebrant containing all that is necessary to be sung or said at services of Holy Eucharist throughout the year.

MISSAL STAND

The stand that holds the Missal.

MISSION

In reference to a congregation, one that is in part dependent upon its Diocese for financial support. (See Parish.)

MITRE

The hat worn by bishops symbolizing what appeared to be tongues of flames over the heads of the disciples on the day of Pentecost, thus representing their apostolic ministry. Pronounced "my-ter."

NARTHEX

The entrance room or area at the rear of the worship space in a Church, where Acolytes, Choir members, and Clergy begin most processions.

NAVE

The area of the Church in which the congregation sits.

OFFICE LIGHTS

Candelabra used during Morning or Evening Prayer.

OFFERING PLATES

The silver, brass, or wood plates used by ushers to collect the money offerings of the congregation. (See Alms Basin.)

OFFICIANT

One who conducts or leads a worship service, other than the Holy Eucharist, such as Morning Prayer or Evening Prayer. (See Celebrant.)

PALL

A square piece of cardboard or plastic covered with white linen, often decorated with lace or other stitching that covers the Chalice before and after the Communion.

PASCHAL CANDLE

A two to three foot-tall candle placed in the Church from Easter until Pentecost. It is usually decorated with Easter symbols, including five wax pins in the shape of a cross, symbolizing the five wounds of Christ. It is also properly lit during baptisms and the Burial Office.

PARISH

The designation given to a congregation that is financially independent.

PATEN

A thin, flat plate, made of the same material as the Chalice, from which the consecrated bread (Host) at the Holy Communion is administered.

PISCINA

A sink that drains directly into the ground, used to reverently dispose of wine that has been consecrated, and to wash vessels used at the Eucharist.

PRAYER DESK

A small desk with a sloping top and a kneeler situated in the Chancel, used by the Officiant during Morning or Evening Prayer services.

PROCESSIONAL CROSS

A cross attached to a five to six foot pole, carried in liturgical processions.

PULPIT

The place, on the Gospel side of the Church, from which the sermon is delivered.

PURIFICATOR

A small, square piece of white Linen used during administration of the Holy Communion to clean the Chalice.

RECTOR

The Ordained Minister, normally a Priest, elected by the Vestry to be the spiritual and administrative leader of a Parish. (See Vicar.)

RECTORY

House or apartment where the Rector lives.

RESERVED SACRAMENT

Consecrated bread and wine that is kept in the Church following the service of Holy Communion, to be distributed to parishioners in hospitals or shut-ins who cannot attend church. Also used for the extended ministry of the deacon, it is normally kept in an Aumbry or Tabernacle.

RETABLE

A shelf or ledge behind the Altar that is used for flowers, candles, and a cross. Churches with free-standing altars do not always have a retable.

REVERENCE

A slight bow toward the Altar made as a gesture of respect and honor to the presence of God in the Church. (See Genuflect.)

ROCHET AND CHIMERE

Special vestments worn only by bishops only. The white chimere is similar to an ankle-length surplice but the sleeves are gathered at the wrists. The red rochet is like a body-length vest.

SACRISTY

Directly off the Sanctuary, the room where sacred vessels, linens, and other related items are kept. It has a sink, called a Piscina, where vessels are washed after services.

SACRISTY BELL

Rung from the Sacristy, the bell informs the congregation that the Celebrant is ready to enter the Sanctuary to begin the Holy Eucharist.

SANCTUARY

The area of the Chancel in which the altar stands. It is usually separated from the Choir by an Altar Rail.

SANCTUARY LAMP

The light (usually a candle within an amber or red glass) that hangs in front of or above the Aumbry or Tabernacle. When lit, it signifies that there is Reserved Sacrament present. In some other traditions it signifies the perpetual presence of Christ in his Church.

SANCTUS BELL

The bell (or bells) rung by an Acolyte at the Sanctus and at other certain points during the Prayer of Consecration.

SERVER

An Acolyte who serves at the altar. "Server" and "Acolyte" are often interchangeable words.

STOLE

A band of cloth worn around the neck, hanging to the knees, or longer by priests and bishops. It is worn over the left shoulder by deacons.

SURPLICE

A white vestment reaching to the knees, with full, open sleeves. It is worn over a Cassock. (See Cotta.)

TABERNACLE

A free-standing box made of wood or metal that rests on the Altar or Retable where the Reserved Sacrament and Holy Oils are kept. (See Aumbry.)

TAPER

A two-foot piece of wick, covered with a thin layer of wax, used in a Candle Lighter to light candles; can also refer to a processional candle.

THURIBLE

The metal or ceramic pot and chain that holds burning Incense; also called a "Censer."

THURIFER

The Acolyte who carries the Thurible.

TORCH

A wooden pole that holds a short, thick candle used for processions.

TORCHBEARER

The Acolyte who carries a Torch.

VEST

To put on Vestments in preparation for a worship service.

VESTMENTS

Any item of clothing that is worn for the purpose of identifying the ministers who lead the worship of the Church. (See Alb, Cassock, Cassock-Alb, Chasuble, Cincture, Cope, Cotta, Girdle, Mitre, Rochet and Chimere, Stole, Surplice.)

VESTRY

The room or area in which service participants Vest, and often where torches and other paraphernalia used during the service are kept; also refers to the group of elected members of a Parish who are responsible for the temporal affairs of the congregation.

VICAR

The Ordained Minister, usually a Priest, who is appointed by the Bishop to be the spiritual and administrative leader of a Mission.

WAFER

A small, flat disk of unleavened bread most often used for Holy Communion. (See Host, Elements.)

Notes

Notes